MW00876880

TABLE OF CONTENTS

ACKNOWLEDGMENTS

I would like to thank my daughter Allyson who started me on this journey of writing, by encouraging me to blog, and my first born Allan who would always say "good for you, mommy." To my husband, Michael, who has taken this journey with me, loving, laughing, and most of the time just shaking his head. Thank you for supporting every new project and idea that God sends my way. You are My Hair... My Marriage.

To my niece, Stefani, who took the time to listen to me and encouraged me "to connect, grow, and change," much love. To my Metamorphosis covenant community, you have walked with me from the very beginning of this ministry; thank you for listening and hearing.

To my circle of sisters, thanks for your encouragement, believing in me, pushing me, and saying "girl you can do this." To Pamela, Carmen, and "queen daughter," Melva, your insight and willingness to speak truth in my life has helped me to grow in a new way. To Lee, and Sonia, thanks for cheering me on and even showing me what it means to embrace one's creative side, no matter what age you are. Terrie, you have been like a midwife in my life always coaching me to push, breathe, and push. To Marion, one of the greatest cheerleaders anyone can have, thank you and Ron for a platform to preach and to share my gifts in an authentic way.

Lenora and Carolyn, the both of you see what I can't see, speak what I refuse to utter, and always believe the impossible for ministry, even for Michael, and me. Thanks for your love and support, especially in this project.

To my sisters who have loved me through every season of my marriage, Clye, Marva, and Priscilla, thanks for loving me unconditionally. To my sister Peggy, your encouragement during a dark period brought light and hope. To the women of Community Church, thank you for always loving me and praying for me, your "Lady Felecia," and to Emma for your willingness to roll up your sleeves and work. To Deboris, thanks for being my dream keeper and always nudging me to make it happen. To my other "Puahs", Virginia, and Jahari, you have helped me by showing me the "how". I am learning to "fly my plane while I am building it."

To Miss Betty, for thirteen years, I sat in your chair, laughing and loving and wondering why "you never based my scalp when I got a perm." Love you! To my sister/stylist, "I can't find nobody to do my hair friend", Pastor Lora Adams King, thanks for letting me sit in your chair and in your heart.

To my extended family, my mother's sisters, "Aunt Mot", "Aunt Cat," and "Cousin Fuzz." You were there from the very beginning. When I look into your faces, I see my mom's spirit. Your love for her was able to carry her through her sickness.

To my blood sisters, Tish, Laine, and Gwen and our dear brother, Ronald, who survived living in a house with a beautician. You started the journey with me "popped" hands and all.

DEDICATION

This book is dedicated to the memory of the one who birthed my journey, my mom, Essie B, your presence and your spirit is always with me. I miss you immensely and wish I had sat a little longer in your chair. And to the memory of my Dad, Ozer Pearson, we were able to do what we do and wear our "do" because of you.

To the late Mr. Timothy Spencer, your love and support is missed, but most of all, your spirit of "we are going to wear our own hair" still resides in my soul.

CHAPTER 1

GOD
OMAN
2 k13

MESSY HEAD

I will celebrate thirty-eight years of marriage on August 30, 2013. My husband still says our anniversary is August 31. Perhaps it is because August 31, 1975, was when we began our new life together as husband and wife.

These days, thirty-eight years is a long time to be married to the same person. My husband always says that "married folks want to be single, and single folks always want to be married." Everyone thinks that the grass is greener on the other side. Is it really green on either side? I guess that is why I see my hair journey like my marriage journey: always changing, never staying the same.

I grew up in a beautician's home. This translates into trying every hairstyle and new do in the world. My journey with styles, cuts, and colors runs parallel to my marriage over the past thirty-eight years. One of my first hairstyles at the age of five was typical of African American girls born in the fifties: two braids in the back and one braid on top.

My mother was notorious for being heavy-handed, and I was known (and still am) for being tender headed. Every morning fresh parts were placed in my head, and my sides were brushed down with Royal Crown hair grease. We always had ribbons in our hair. My day always started with a fresh a hairdo, but by the end of the school day, the sides were fuzzy. The ribbons were loose, and the braids were doing their own thing, going north, south, east, and west. I was not preoccupied as a five-year-old with keeping every hair in place. My messy head was usually an indication of the type of day I'd had. Some days were good, and some days were not so good.

My marriage in the early years was like the hairstyle of a five-year-old. We worked so hard to have everything in place. But no one prepared us for the times when things would unravel because we were not perfect. We thought that if we could just start out with all the right stuff, we would not have many problems.

In our first year of marriage, we lived in a three-room basement apartment that was a part of my husband's parents' home. I was a full-time student in seminary, and I had no clue about what it meant to be a wife, a lover, and a friend. I am not sure how we juggled having all of our emotional needs met by each other. In those early years of marriage, it was probably more about the physical part of the relationship (sex). I found myself in bed with this man every morning, saying to myself, "I never knew that morning breath could be this bad." Quantity was key, even if it meant neglecting the deeper conversations that should have been taking place. What did we know? We were still learning about each other, and I had no idea how to ask for what I needed. I had never lived with anyone other than my three sisters and a college roommate.

Like that earnest, hopeful five-year-old on the way to kindergarten, we thought that we would return home with every ribbon and part in place.

Marriage is work, and how tender headed you are will determine not what you will endure, but how you will endure it. I decided that I liked having my hair look a certain way; therefore, I was willing to go through getting my hand popped by the infamous black comb. I also decided that I wanted my marriage to flourish; therefore, I was willing to go through the process of having my heart stretched and my mind challenged for growth and change.

At the end of my day as a five-year-old, my hair was definitely not in place, but it was manageable. In those early years of my marriage, many things were not in place, but they were manageable. We were on our way, with loose ribbons, fuzzy edges, and definitely a messy head.

CHAPTER 2
IN THE KITCHEN

GOD
OMAN
ZK13

IN THE KITCHEN

There are some who say that when a person invites you into his or her home and you sit at their kitchen table, you have moved from being a guest to a friend. The kitchen table is where bonding takes place and barriers are broken down.

The kitchen in a beautician's home, however, means something totally different. The term *kitchen* refers to that place at the back of your head, otherwise called the nape. For me, it was a tender spot where my curls, kinks, and tangled hair came together to irritate me.

The kitchen was also that room where I sat between my mother's legs in a chair with her best friend, the straightening comb. I still cringe when I think of that hot comb going into my own personal kitchen. I never understood why my mother called it the kitchen. Perhaps in the pre-relaxer days, it was the place where the most heat was applied.

Growing up in a beautician's family, I came to understand that there was always a process to doing hair. Usually it started in the kitchen. My mother's philosophy was that if the kitchen was straightened, the rest of the hair was easy to do. You might ask, "Who looks at a person's neck?" I believe that there was wisdom in starting at the nape to ensure a good-looking hairstyle. Even today as I sit in the salon, my stylist still starts at the base of my neck.

Every marriage has a kitchen—that is, a place where the real work must begin. I have found that when you take care of the basic things in your marriage, such as unconditional love, communication, finances, trust, and even the commitment that "I am in this for the long haul," you will find that the kitchen can also become that place of warmth, ease, and growth. I confess that I am tender headed, and things that don't bother most people often cause me a lot of discomfort. Even in my marriage, I have often wanted to avoid that part of the relationship that caused me discomfort; however, I knew that it was necessary for my marriage to grow and develop.

Then it happened—that is, our first fight. It felt like the hot comb against the edges of the nape of my hair. I cannot tell you what our first major fight was about, but what I remember was that it felt like the kitchen in our three-room apartment. I was yelling, and he was yelling. He was not going to tell me what to do, and he definitely would not raise his voice at me. Of course, my version is the one for this book.

I said," I am leaving, and I don't have to take this."

My husband said, " I don't care and you can go."

We only had one car, and it was his. So I called a taxi and asked to be taken to my parents' home. I rang the doorbell, and my father answered the door. "Essie B, she's back."

"Daddy could you pay the taxi driver?" I asked. "I don't have the money."

I entered my parent's home and sat in the kitchen. My mom asked me what was wrong. I told her my version of the fight. She looked at me and said, "Chile, is that all?"

Thirty minutes later the phone rang. My mom answered the telephone. "It is Michael."

Forty-five minutes later the doorbell was ringing. My dad said, "It's him."

We talked at the kitchen table, and I returned to my three-room apartment. Thirty-eight years later, we are still talking, but now I don't leave—at least not the house.

Thirty-eight years is also a long time to both be in the kitchen and work on the kitchen. Life's challenges sometimes seem like my mom's best friend, the straightening comb—heated, but necessary for a finished product. I have come to realize that it wasn't so bad being in the kitchen. Eventually, I moved from the chair between my mother's legs to the table, where we talked about how nice my hair looked and how I was doing as a new wife. In those earlier years of marriage, we would not have made it if it had not been for the work done in the kitchen.

CHAPTER 3
MY FIRST PERM

MY FIRST PERM

The first of anything can be exciting as well as challenging. I remember wanting to figure out that life had to be more than a hot comb, a jar of blue hair grease, and wishing that the weather would always remain sunny and dry. This was the life of a girl who clearly was tender headed, whose mother was heavy-handed, and who hated getting her hair combed and pressed.

In 1967 my beautician mom wanted to try a new technique for straightening my hair. I am sure she felt like I did about doing my hair. My crying days would soon be over, and her days of having to wrestle with me would be ending soon as well. I was so excited because now I would not have to endure all that a press and comb would require. My life was getting ready to change. I would be free, and most of all, my hand would not get popped by the big, black comb.

I was in ninth grade. I remember being in my mother's beauty shop waiting for my life to change. I do not remember the name of my first perm, and I can't remember the entire process. But I do remember some burning. I asked myself, "Burning? What had I traded for the straight look?" Nevertheless, I was on my way to hair that could withstand the weather and water.

The hair dryer now replaced the straightening comb. It seemed like it took my hair forever to dry, not to mention the pins that hold the rollers in place, which went into my scalp. It hurt like the devil!

I find it very interesting that whether the hot comb or the white cream, nothing is ever as easy as it seems. There is always a price to pay for looking good. With the hot comb, the price was detangling—Lord knows what that was like if my hair dried before my mother was finished!

With the perm it meant some burning and a very long time sitting under the dryer. I understood that a chemical treatment was really a process, and no step could be skipped for the sake of time. Which was better or easier? At that time, I was sure that it was the perm.

Sometimes in marriage, we become disgruntled with the way things are going and feel that there has to be an easier way. I felt that way about my first perm. I believed that life could be easier. I soon understood that no matter what you do to your hair, it is still a process.

A good marriage is also a process. Better communication in a marriage is a process.

Forgiveness in marriage is a process. Stronger communication in a marriage is a process. Nothing is easy! I thought moving from the hot comb to the relaxer cream would solve all of my problems, but there was still me. I was the one thing in the entire equation that had not changed.

Nothing is easy in marriage. It requires work, love, and the ability to push through some difficult stuff. Marriage loves unconditionally. Sometimes it may require working through the pain, which is part of the process. Marriage, like hair, requires making a decision about what you are willing to go through to get the end result. This means time, the right support, and the willingness to see it through.

Marriage requires a commitment to the process of being emotionally and spiritually healthy. For me, this means creating an environment that encourages open communication. My first perm at the age of fourteen was the beginning of a long hair journey with the white cream. My saying "I do" was the beginning of a long love journey with my mate. I have always been determined to stay in the "chair" and under the "dryer," no matter how long it takes.

CHAPTER 4
MY AFRO

MY AFRO

I am a product of the seventies. I graduated from high school in the seventies. I finished college in the seventies, and I married in the seventies. I graduated from seminary in the seventies, and I had my first child in the seventies. This was also the time that I came out of the kitchen, out of the chair, and decided that I was going to grow out my perm and wear an Afro.

This was when my mother and I parted company. She could not understand how someone whose hair had to be wetted before it could be combed out wanted to wear it in its natural state. I was a new woman with a new hairdo and a new attitude, so I thought. For me, wearing my Afro would represent freedom and the decision to look really cool, at least for a moment.

Maintaining my Afro was more work than I had anticipated. I did not have the luxury of picking it out and going on about my business. It required special products and braiding it at night. My Afro required combing (yeah), which was a problem, because as I've mentioned before, I am tender headed. You see, no matter what, nothing is ever as easy as it looks. I marveled at the heroines of the seventies with their sexy "big hair." My hair would never stand up like what I saw on the screen and in *Ebony* or *Jet* magazines.

My mom wanted me to cut it because she was not feeling the "big hair." But I was not going to listen to the queen of the straightening comb and white cream. What did she know about where I was with my hair, my life, and my look?

As I was reflecting about the Afro and the correlation of this hairstyle with my marriage, I remember a silly fight with my husband over who was going to pay for lunch. The fight had started in the car on the way to a restaurant— though at that point it had nothing to do with lunch at all but rather something about a phone conversation. All I know is that I was angry and so was he.

I thought about my Afro in the seventies. I thought about all the work that it took for me to maintain a look that was supposed to represent freedom and the ability to go with the flow. I thought about the fact that, just as my wonderful Afro took a lot of work to maintain, so would my marriage.

Often the real work is not in the big things but in the small things—the small things that can really set you off, out of nowhere. You look across the table and say to yourself,

"Harpo, who dat man?" You may have let go of the chemicals, but there are products that you still need for your hair to look healthy and have that special Afro sheen.

My marriage is like my Afro: it may look easy to others on the outside but requires a lot of work. I am glad for the work that has been put into it because when we are at lunch and have a falling out, over God knows what, I am able to remember that he is my friend, my lover, and the father of my children. I am able to then smile (not immediately) and say, "Ise married now."

CHAPTER 5
CORN ROWS

CORNROWS

Finishing college in the seventies was a time of personal growth in my life. I was learning whom I was and what I wanted to do with my life. I thought that it was the best time to figure it all out. Lessons from life, love, and of course hair would mean trying something old, yet something new. I was evolving, and even today, I am not sure what my cornrow journey was all about.

It is interesting to me that that every major change in my early years started either in my mother's chair or sitting on the floor between her legs, getting a new do or updating an old one. Every time I walked through the door, my mom's instinct would let her know that she and I were in for another hair adventure. At that time, it would be cornrows that would display my mother's artistic ability with hair.

There are some things that never go away with time or age. That day I discovered that if you were tender headed at ages two, six, and sixteen, you would be tender headed at age twenty as well. I must have forgotten that not only was I tender headed, but also I was now in the grip of the heavy-handed queen of "girl, you better hold your head straight." I am not sure where the black comb was, but she still had the power of yanking your head in the position that she wanted it in for the style that she was creating.

I realized that day that cornrows were beautiful when they were completed, but they required a new kind of tenacity. This process was intricate. It required braiding the hair close to the scalp, using an underhanded, upward motion. There was not a break in the process until you came to the end of the row. I was committed to having this really cool hairstyle, but I wanted to cry. I wanted it to come to an end quickly. But it would need to be completed because my mom was a beautician who always finishes a job.

An hour later that Sunday afternoon, it was done. It was tight, and I had a headache. But it was complete. Tight, painful, but beautiful. When I returned back to college, I did not talk about the process for the tender-headed sister who wanted cornrows. I wore them with pride, headache and all.

Isn't that just like marriage? Sometimes we admire other couples from afar. We think to ourselves, "What a wonderful marriage!" We notice all the things they do for each other. We marvel at how they smile at each other when they are in each other's presence.

Sometimes if we are not careful, we can look over at our spouse and think, "I wish he or she would do better and be better." We only see what we see and never understand the depth and intricate process that another couple may have gone through to get to where they are now. Their warm smiles might have come from years of struggle and questioning their love and commitment. Their physical touching and embracing might be from working to stay connected emotionally through disappointments and failures in the marriage.

Being in a clergy, marriage is a good example of people not understanding what life can be like. It is more than sitting on the first or second row of the church. For me, it meant working through my stuff, while trying to handle other people's stuff. Many times it was painful, but necessary. Marriage is work, and being married to a pastor is more work.

Marriage is also a process; like the corn-rows that are braided close to the scalp, there are things that happen in a marriage that are close to the heart—betrayal, misunder-standings, not being heard or feeling valued. However, if a couple decides that they are willing to go through the process so that the marriage can be better, then they will be one of those couples that is admired from afar. Someone will say, "Wow, they look so happy and contented."

I am often reminded of the price I paid that day for those cornrows. For me, it was painful but worth it. Like my cornrows experi-ence, those who admire from afar will never know the price that was paid to look good.

CHAPTER 6
JHERI CURL

MY JHERI CURL

Whoever had the bright idea of going through the tedious process of "rearranging" your hair to get a glossy (greasy), loosely curled look? Such a look would require placing several rods in your hair and then putting all of this liquid solution on each rod. Although I was looking for an easier process (always), this new look would also require sitting under the dryer and wetting the hair all over again. Needless to say, when I left the salon, I would have to wear a plastic cap to keep the water from dripping down my back. Why would I want a Jheri curl?

Perhaps it was because I had this vision in my mind of curly hair that would look like that of the women on *The Cosby Show* or *A Different World,* or like that of Michael Jackson. I thought the Jheri curl would be my solution to a natural but curly look. OK, by now, you know that I have a fixation with hair. I will try every latest thing that's out in the salon.

I started my Jheri curl journey by first cutting off all of my permed hair. My mother gave me my first "cold wave." She was just as bad as I was, always looking for an opportunity to try out a new product or new style. The Jheri curl was not a very flattering hairstyle for me, but I was determined to move toward a process that promised curly hair. What was I thinking? You see, the secret to this look was not in what was done to the hair in the salon. It was in the activator spray that was required every day in order for your curl pattern to show.

The only problem with the activator was that it was greasy. Your hair would be dry and look like an Afro if you did not use the curl activator. You got up in the morning, and you used your activator. You used it at night, and you definitely used it after you shampooed your hair. The activator was true to its name: it activated the curl. As I think about one of my least favorite hairstyles, I realize that a Jheri curl was not a Jheri curl without the greasy (glossy) activator.

Marriage has those years that are really great. It also has those years when you say to yourself, "What was I thinking to go through all of these changes?" The Jheri curl stage of marriage can come when children arrive on the scene. When I was pregnant, I am told that I was not the easiest person to get along with. Who wants love and affection when there is a whole person inside of you, kicking and moving around?

During this Jheri curl stage of my marriage, we definitely needed the activator. There were sleepless nights and long days. Children will zap all the moisture from your relationship if you are not careful. Our first-born was a joy, but I should have known that we were in for a change when he was born during an ice storm (in Atlanta). I had the flu, and he came to us with a fever. I needed the activator. Our life would never be the same. I wanted sleep, rest, sleep, and more sleep. My husband wanted sex, sex, sex, and more sex.

You wonder, could my life have been better in another state—that is, single with no children? Then you look in the mirror, and you say, "Oh my God, I forgot my activator." Clearly, when you are in the Jheri curl stage of marriage, you need the activator.

You may need to activate patience, listening, trust, unconditional love, faith, and even hope. You might just need to activate romance. Remember the long kisses that you use to give your spouse at the end of a long day?

The Jheri curl hairdo was short-lived for me. It was of those hairstyles that I never returned to. If you are in a Jheri curl stage in your marriage, get the activator out. It may be greasy, but you will find that it is necessary in order for the curl pattern to show. Your curl pattern of love is waiting for the activator.

CHAPTER 7
LEAVE IT TO THE EXPERTS

LEAVE IT TO THE EXPERTS

I have always been one of those girls who would follow people through a store just to figure out what they were wearing in their hair or what they'd done to it. I usually don't have a problem with this because of my southern roots. Being from the South, I will strike up a conversation with just about anyone. Once you have given me the information, I will always try to find an inexpensive way to get it done. Some people would say today that I was cheap, but I call it wanting to look like Hollywood on a Norwood budget.

It's true that I have had an ongoing affair with hair all of my life. But this time I fell hard. I fell in love with extensions. I had to have them. I wanted that beautiful, curly, wavy, full head of hair. I would fantasize about this hairstyle as I watched *A Different World* and *Living Single* in the late nineties. How could I get this hairstyle? And then a woman walked into church. She had the type of hair that I wanted. She was wearing the style that I wanted. God was with me that day. God heard my prayer and gave me the desire of having that beautiful head of hair. After much discussion, the woman stated that although she did not do her own hair, she could do my hair. All I had to do was buy the hair!

I was now off to buy packs of hair. I had the vision; she had the skill and expertise. I was on my way to having a head of hair that would at least have me looking like…never mind. I should have known that I was in trouble when it took her only two hours to do my hair. This process requires tiny braids, and it usually requires at least four hours.

When I got up out of the chair in my family room, I wanted to cry. My head did not look like what I had envisioned. It looked like a recently plowed field that was being prepared for planting. You could see every part and the place where each extension was braided to the hair. It did not look like her head. I thanked her, gave her a holy hug, said good-bye, and cried. What would I do? I was going out of town on Monday, and it was already Saturday evening. I would need to call my hairstylist, swallow my pride, and see if she could fix this mess or at least take it out.

When I arrived at her shop that night, she shook her head and asked, "What were you trying to accomplish? Who did you use to accomplish this? And what were you thinking?" She called in one of her stylists, who stated that he would come over on Monday morning and work his magic for me. He would try to make me presentable before I left for my trip. It would not be a *Different World* look, but at least it would be an improvement. He rescued me, and I learned a valuable lesson: leave it to the experts who are licensed, trained, and experienced in their profession.

In marriage there will be times that you hit a cycle of problems that your girlfriend, mother, sister, boyfriend, or best "boo" cannot help you with. There may come a time when you need to find professional help. It is the big *C*—not cancer, but counseling. Some things in our marriages will require "sitting on the couch." There is no shame in doing this. It is realizing that God has people who are called, trained, and equipped to help us navigate through deep waters when we are in trouble.

When we are facing problems in our relationships and marriages, don't be afraid to make that phone call and say you need help.

I learned a valuable lesson that weekend that put me back in my trained stylist's chair. They were able to clean up what I had messed up.

There will be times in our marriages when we need help to restore, renew, and refresh. There will be times when we need help straightening out things that we have messed up, but please leave it to the experts!

CHAPTER 8
WHOA OR WEAVE

GOD
OMAN 2K13

WHOA OR WEAVE

When you consider yourself a hair diva, you spend a lot of your time trying to figure what people have in their hair. Sometimes in the midst of your hallelujah in church, you find yourself saying, "Oh, God, I praise you. But I wonder, what color is that in her hair?" I have found myself being hugged by a mother of the church and wondered as she patted me on the head: Was she trying to see if I had a weave or was wearing a wig? I must admit that in my heart I always wanted a weave, but my status as a tender-headed girl (now woman) always comes back to haunt me.

Then one day, to my amazement, I heard about clip-ons. I could now have the added hair without sewing it in. Why would I go to such lengths for hair? I can't really answer this question; I can only say that it was a part of my hair journey. I bought the clips and sewed them to the weft of the hair. It was painless, and I was happy.

Here is the key: clip-on hair is a temporary fix. A clip-on is not intended to sustain a long-term permanent solution for hair extensions. Day in and day out of putting these metal clips into my hair caused significant breakage. You would think that I would have learned by now. No, I wanted an immediate fix for what I felt was necessary at the time. However, the clips eventually failed me.

Later, with the advent of bonded hair glue, my hope was restored. I would now be free. The hair would lie flat. Now when the church mother prayed for me and wanted to console me, she would not feel the metal clips and definitely not any tracks. God is faithful; however, there is no easy process when it comes to hair.

When I visited my mother that summer, I was so excited about my newfound solution, but it was time to take the glue-ridden hair out. I needed a relaxer (at a reduced rate, of course). To my surprise, I did not realize that the glue remover available in the hair supply store would not be sufficient enough to remove the hair.

So we did what any southern beautician would do. My mother got out the jar of Vaseline and saturated the tracks. The hair came out, along with some of my own hair. My head was sore from all of the pulling, and I needed a relaxer to cover up the damage. I paid a dear price for beauty that day.

My mom's famous words resounded in my ear: "Girl, when are you going to stop trying everything and let your hair do what it needs to do and wants to do—grow?" I was a hair junkie, and I could not stop—or would not stop. We got through the process but not without a price. There were some broken pieces of hair and a few chemical burns that left in time, but I learned my lesson. Nothing is as easy as it seems, and nothing comes without a price.

Isn't that just like marriage? There are things that we want in our marriages, such as a fuller relationship, better communication, more intimacy, and even more fulfilling sex.

Like many people, I am guilty of wanting quick solutions and temporary fixes. So we go away for the weekend but never deal with the real issues in the marriage. We get a new piece of jewelry but will not address what we're really thinking about. We go out with our friends, laugh, and have a great time, but never ask, "How are you really doing? How can I support the both of you?"

Although getaway weekends are great, a new piece of jewelry is wonderful. And while time with friends is important, long-term solutions to our marital problems are still key. If they are left unattended, we become frustrated, and just like the experience of removing the glue from my hair, there is breakage and burning. Nothing substitutes for emotional health in a marriage.

For years I thought it was OK to blame my partner if I was unhappy. Like my clip-on hair and glue, blaming my spouse made me feel better, but that feeling was temporary. Temporary fixes in marriage are just that. My marriage needed more than a temporary fix. It needed a more permanent solution, which meant taking the words of my mother to heart: "Girl, when are you going to stop trying everything and let your hair do what it needs to do and wants to do—grow?"

I am committed to having a healthy marriage. I am aware that there is a price that will be paid. Long-term sustainable marriages are not built on quick fixes but on processes that lead to health and wholeness. I have made a commitment to love my spouse, communicate what I need, allow God to work on me, and allow the marriage to do what it wants to do—grow.

CHAPTER 9
THE BUN

GOD
OMAN 2K13

THE BUN

On August 30, 2005, I celebrated thirty years of marriage. The hairstyle that stands out in my mind as I celebrated this anniversary was the bun. Why the bun? It is the hairstyle that I wore when I needed to get to the salon. Often, I was complimented on how my bun gave me a look of distinction and sophistication. There was no real secret to this hairstyle. It only required a strong brush and some gel.

There was a season in my life when I had to wear the bun. It was not because I could not get to the salon. It was when the person in my life who popped my hands with the black comb, who straightened my edges, who gave me my first perm and the Jheri curl, and who rolled her eyes every time I decided that I needed to try something different, was now ill.

My beautician had pancreatic cancer and was fighting for her life. Now my trip to the salon took on new meaning. All of a sudden, my hair was not growing. It was breaking in spots, which required that I do something different to hide the patches. Thus the bun became my hairstyle of choice during that difficult time. I was grieving, and my grief was manifesting itself through the loss of my hair. I thought that I was OK. I was still smiling and giving everyone the church talk. Internally, my heart was breaking. Now I was losing the one who had started me on this hair journey. On June 16, 1995, my mother, my friend, and my beautician died.

I remember returning to Pennsylvania, where I was living at the time. I sat in my stylist's chair and took down my bun. My stylist noticed that the spots that were previously weak and brittle and that would not grow, now had new growth. My mother had transitioned and so had my hair. It was coming back, saying that it was OK to grieve and to acknowledge the loss. My hair was grieving for the one who took care of the messy head, who had straightened out the kitchen, who put the cornrows in, and who had rolled her eyes at the Afro.

You may ask yourself how this is related to my marriage, as I reflect on my thirtieth wedding anniversary. My twenty-ninth year of marriage was a very difficult year for my husband and me. We were faced with challenges that we had never encountered. My husband and I went through things that caused the both of us to grieve. We were grieving from the loss of trust and faith we'd had in one another. We were committed to see it through and work out our stuff. Working out our stuff meant that we needed to sit with the sadness of the brokenness in our relationship, acknowledge that we were in pain, and learn to navigate to a place of healing.

The ability to grieve is necessary when you have loss in your life. It is also necessary when there is loss in a marriage. We were transitioning and eventually returning to health and wholeness as a couple.

I lost my mother and grieved, but I was able to hold on to her memory and the memories of our talks in the kitchen, talks over the shampoo bowl, and the talks in her chair.

In marriage, I have been able to do the same when things were difficult. During that difficult period, I was able to remember a kind and loving person that I had fallen in love with. I was able to reflect on how far God had brought us. Today, if you are in a marriage or relationship that may be in trouble, never give up.

You see, the bun is good some of the time. It was essential for me during those months that my mother was dying; however, I am told by many stylists that it is not good to pull your hair back all the time. Too much pulling can cause breakage. One day, I decided that it was time to take the bun down, and when I did, the new growth had already begun.

In marriage, it is not good to pull back and away from one another when life becomes difficult. Staying connected and not allowing pain to separate you will require more work, but in the end you will have a smile in your heart and eventually on your face.

CHAPTER 10
MY FRENCH ROLL

MY FRENCH ROLL

I come from a family of four sisters and one brother. My brother managed to survive in a family of girls with a father who was quiet and a mother who had a strong hand and a strong will. My brother was a lot like my father, and despite being exposed to a lot of hairstyles, I never remember my brother giving his opinion about any of them—until one summer when I was visiting my family in Atlanta.

I was home and I was happy. I had found a hairstyle that required very little maintenance and would last from one salon visit to the next.

My brother looked at me and said, "I don't like your hair. Why is it so hard? You must have a ton of gel in your hair." Unfortunately, my feelings were hurt somewhat, but it caused me to take a hard look at my hard French roll.

He asked, "Aren't you the president and CEO of an organization?"

I replied, "You know I am."

Then he began to say more about my hard French roll. He used the word *ghetto*, which was really OK, because that was where we were from and, needless to say, where he hung out. I am not sure why my hard French roll caused such a stir in my silent brother, but it did, and he did not like it on his sister.

If you have read this far in this book, you know that there is always some correlation with my hair journey to my marriage. I was shocked because my brother had seen many hairstyles. Of course—his mother was a beautician. Did what he say stop me from wearing my hard French roll? Of course not. I eventually transitioned out of the hard French roll, not because of what he said but because the trend had changed.

Later I tried to reclaim my hard French roll. I had moved to Atlanta after my mother died, and I no longer had the opportunity to sit in her chair and laugh and be talked about and talk about others. I had found a new stylist, Tim, whom I'd grown to love. He was my friend, and he was willing to take my hair journey with me. He would speak life into my hair and tell me the truth.

I had an appointment and wanted to bring my hard French roll back to life. Tim said to me, "I don't do hard hair."

I asked, "What?"

He explained, "Hard hair is the lazy woman's hairstyle. Your problem is that you don't want to do anything to your hair, and besides, putting all that gel on your hair week after week is not good for it in the long run. By the way, that is not what I do."

I was shocked and appalled. The nerve of him telling me what he would or would not do for me. After all, I was paying him. He went on to say, "If you want a French roll, we can make that happen, but it will not be plastered with gel. It will last probably a couple of days, but that is it. Now sit yourself down and let's move on with getting you out of here!"

I sat down and said, "That's OK, because if it is not going to be hard, I don't want it."

He said, "Lazy—that is what you are. Let's keep this hair healthy. When we do this, people will stop you and comment on your hair. After all, my name is attached to anything that I do. When you leave my chair, you are representing me."

I never asked for another hard French roll, ponytail, or anything that would require gel. I loved my stylist because he spoke truthfully to me that day. He set me straight in so many ways that when he passed, there was a void my life.

Both my stylist's personal assessment of my hard French roll and my brother's displeasure with it speak volumes to me as they relate to marriage. My brother felt that my look was a reflection of the crowd that he hung out with, and my stylist said that it was the lazy woman's hairstyle and could cause damage over a long period of time. One was concerned about the exterior (appearance) and the other the interior (health of the hair).

In marriage, should we be concerned about what image we display to others, or should we focus on the interior, that is, the emotional and spiritual health of our relationship?

If you are in a fishbowl relationship—that is, you or your spouse has a public life—I would say that the two couldn't be separated. The interior work in marriage requires understanding who we are, what experiences we bring to the marriage, and how our family origins impact us. The exterior work in a marriage includes things like communication, finances, support, spending time together, intentional date nights, and just holding hands for no reason at all.

My stylist spoke the truth about taking the lazy way out rather than working on the health of the hair. This also holds true for marriage. Marriage is work, and it requires a daily commitment that we will make it, if we choose to.

There have been days when I pondered, "How did I find myself in this place?"

Then God would whisper in my ear, "You are still in the chair, and your process is not over."

Appearance was important to my brother; for my stylist, it was more about the health of the hair. Both were right. My public life must reflect who I really am and not be based on a trend or fashion. Also, if I take care of myself emotionally and spiritually, my authentic self will be present in my relationship. This can only happen when I allow God to work on me daily. I am committed to not being lazy in my life and in my marriage. I am willing to do the work—are you?

CHAPTER 11
MY WIGS

GOD
MAN 2K13

MY WIGS

I have a room with wigs in it. It is a part of a collection that I have acquired over the years. Some are human, and many are synthetic. My mother used to say: "Every woman needs at least one wig in her wardrobe." I took this to heart—especially the "at least" part. Wigs were fun, and I would make my friends upset because I did not care who knew that it was a wig. I called the wigs my girlfriends. They were my go-to solution between hair appointments.

I was always drawn to the big, curly-hair wigs. They made feel happy and empowered;

however, it was good to know that at the end of the day, I could take them off. After all, they were just wigs. People would ask me, "Why do you wear a wig? You have such beautiful hair." I responded by quoting my mom. Those people who had been with me on my hair journey knew that it was what I did. I was not obligated to wear wigs every day.

Once, at my old job, we were having an outdoor party, and there were singers on the stage. People were throwing things, such as shoes, keys, and hats, and saying, "You better sing." In the spirit of fun, I took my wig off and threw it on the stage. I have since left that job (not because I took off my wig).

I am told that people are still talking about the woman who threw her wig on the stage. We laughed so hard. I went and picked up my wig and placed it back on my head and finished eating my burger! The great thing about a wig is that you can put it on or take it off, if you don't take it too seriously. It is just what it is—a wig held on by two hairpins.

There are things in your marriage that, if you are not careful, can drown out your laughter and kill your joy. You might forget about the fun that you had when you first met. You might forget that it is OK to be yourself, and you can say and do whatever you want with this person that you said, "I do" to.

Sometimes we take ourselves too seriously. We forget about the things that cause us to have a belly laugh. We must still reclaim and maintain our laughter. Some things in our marriage should be treated like the wig I took off and threw on the stage—not that seriously. It was unexpected, and it was fun.

Sometimes marriage requires taking some things off and throwing them away, such as anger, disappointment, and frustration. I am the funny one in our relationship, but what tickles me about my partner is that he laughs at his own jokes. I am amazed, but when I hear him laugh, it makes me laugh.

I know you might feel that there is not much to laugh about these days, but somewhere, behind the pain and hurt, ask God to crack open a window for you so that you can laugh, even if it means laughing at yourself. Yes, my wigs make me feel happy, because they are so easy to handle. Only two hairpins hold them together. They can come off at my pleasure.

My marriage these days makes me feel happy, and it brings me joy to walk with my partner. We had some days when we took ourselves too seriously, and there were some days when we were not serious enough. It was like a synthetic wig on some days and a human wig on other days. Regardless, a wig is still a wig.

Today, I celebrate with the same gut-wrenching laughter that we all experienced that day when the wig came off at the party. I am still loving and laughing and living my life with my partner of thirty-eight years.

CHAPTER 12

it's

NATURAL

IT'S NATURAL

I sat in the chair of a new stylist whom I had not been with for very long. My mom was gone. I no longer lived near Ms. Betty, and Tim had died. I was beginning my metamorphosis to the next stage of my life, like a caterpillar looking forward to evolving into a butterfly.

I found myself saying the words that I thought that I would never say: "I do not want another relaxer." Then I asked myself, "Did I really just say that?" I had always been the one who praised God for the modern creation of lye and other chemicals. How did I get here?

I will give credit to my daughter, who began her natural process with trying to lock, cutting her hair, and starting all over. She was bold and brave enough to cut her shoulder-length hair and step over to the other side. Was this my daughter? I must admit that I loved the idea that my daughter had hair of length because I could not cornrow. So the fact that it had some length made it easy for me to comb every day. Also, she was not tender headed.

After her first year of seminary, she said, "I am not getting a relaxer any longer." I saw her reclaim her natural hair, a texture that I had long forgotten existed. I had allowed her to get her first relaxer at eleven. Later, when she asked me why I'd allowed to her to get a relaxer, I told her that I felt it was the rite of passage for every black girl.

And so I had a conversation with my stylist about what going natural would mean for me. Initially it meant just continuing to go to the shop; then one day the conversation shifted. I said to my new stylist and friend, "I want to wear it short."

She replied, "If you wear it short, you will need a texturizer."

I said, "No, it will be OK." She continued to press it out.

Finally I told her, "I want you to cut it all off." In the natural world of hair, this is called the "big chop."

I did it, and it was freeing. I wondered, "What will my husband say?" I had made a decision, and I liked my decision. I never looked back. I wanted natural hair, but little did I know that like everything else, it would require my learning about what products to use and how to care for my hair. And so my journey began anew!

My daughter was very helpful in guiding me through this difficult stage. She would say, "Mom, this is what you need to do so that you can establish your routine for keeping your hair moisturized." I must say what a wonderful mentor she has been in this stage of my hair journey. I must have bought every curl-definition cream, hair moisturizer, and conditioner in the store. As a hair junkie, I felt myself relapsing.

I began to learn more about my natural hair. The first thing that I discovered was that I had three different textures in my head. Now I realized why I would cry and get my hand popped whenever my mother got to the back of my head—that's where I have the tightest curl. The top is much easier to manage. I also discovered that even though my hair was natural, it still needed to be healthy and maintained. There was just no easy way around what my mom had said—allow the hair to do what it wants to do, grow—and what Tim had said: "We want healthy hair." I can say that is what my hair and marriage journeys have been all about—health and growth.

There was a period in my marriage when I needed to face some issues. Facing these issues would require us working through a process and going for the "big chop." In marriage, this big chop translates into getting rid of all those things in our marriage that were false and draining and that were not bringing us life.

My marriage has had its share of issues, problems, joys, ups, and downs. As with a butterfly, there has to be a metamorphosis. In our case, we were like two caterpillars moving along in life, raising children and doing ministry. Then one day, in order for us to grow, we went through a very painful stage. In the life of a butterfly, it is called the chrysalis. It is in this stage that transformation takes place. The caterpillar tissues are broken down, and the adult structures are formed. We had to be broken down so that who we were as individuals and as a couple could be formed.

It was painful, but it was transforming. I did not like the process, but looking back, it was a much-needed process. I remember asking, "Is all this necessary?" Then my mother's spirit would nudge me along, and I would remember those talks in the kitchen. I would remember her sayings about hair and about life. I would then get a second wind and say that we could do this, and then one day, the change came. Since then, love has sustained us and given us hope.

My natural hair journey began the day that I told my stylist that I did not want another relaxer. My journey of a sustainable, healthy marriage began the day that I decided to accept the fact that all marriages require work and a commitment to one another to make it work. My marriage is a testimony that no matter how long you have been on this journey, there is still room for growth. I am still learning, but I am much farther ahead than where I started.

My hair is natural. Sometimes I wear it straight, but it's natural. My marriage is healthier. Sometimes we get off track, but it is still healthier! My hair...my marriage: what a journey.

23965592R00057

Made in the USA
Charleston, SC
08 November 2013